Ocean Hearts

Published by Brolga Publishing Pty Ltd
ABN 46 063 962 443
PO Box 12544
A'Beckett St
Melbourne, VIC, 8006
Australia

email: markzocchi@brolgapublishing.com.au

National Library of Australia
Cataloguing-in-Publication data
Nimasha Weerakoon, author.
ISBN 9780648327745 (paperback)

A catalogue record for this book is available from the National Library of Australia

Printed in Australia
Cover design by Alice Cannet
Typesetting by Elly Cridland

All attempts have been made to contact the artist of the 'Ocean Heart'.

BE PUBLISHED

Publish through a successful publisher. National Distribution, Dennis Jones & Associates
International Distribution to the United Kingdom, North America.
Sales Representation to South East Asia
Email: markzocchi@brolgapublishing.com.au

Ocean Hearts

N Dumindi

for my lighthouse keepers
(these tides could not have been written without you)

for my ocean heart
(and the stubbornness of waves)

& for you
(i hope the words become rivers)

Contents

Breaking

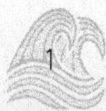

i grew up coloured

in shades of shame

from the brown of my skin

to the shadows of my curves

(i was taught this doubt)

there are days

i am a fragile heart

with quivering skin

and bones that do not

want to hold me

it's a shaking thing

trying to hold the ocean inside of you

to calm it

tame it

not to let it swallow you whole

some days it beats you

that's what they don't understand

some days you are drowning

they just can't see the water

there is an emptiness in me

that i cannot explain

(madness is born in the search for reason)

some days my anxiety

folds itself into my pocket

a familiar weight that i hold

a settling constant

other days it unravels

binding my bones

it paralyses me

an overwhelming force

there is a wobbling

somewhere in the night

like the world has shifted off centre

and i've been walking tilted

ever since

(sometimes living feels wrong)

how do you tell someone

you're drowning and still

expect them to love you

full of seawater?

how do you explain

that the air you've been breathing

all your life suddenly feels like

it belongs to someone else

and with every breath

you're committing a crime?

some hurt

crawls inside your chest

and makes a home there

she was shaking fingers

and a pocketful of apologies

carrying the broken pieces

of her heart like wilting

flowers with no vase

for the girls like me

who locked away their wild

before they even knew

it existed

i hope you never stop

searching for the right key

tonight

the tears spill

pulling the air

just out of reach

and suddenly

i am gasping

drowning

sinking

how quickly this floating

can turn to drowning

i'm afraid these lungs of mine

have not yet learned

how to breathe underwater

i cannot tell

if i don't feel anything

or if i feel everything

and that uncertainty is a friction

i do not understand how to hold

it is quiet

the way hearts break

it is the kind of silence

that aches

i'm swallowing my ghosts

down by the mouthful

tangled up in tasteless truths

that refuse to slide comfortably

down my throat

mine is a haunting

i do not know how to undo

it convinced its way into my blood

this worthlessness

and with it brought

the kind of self-cruelty that

gripped my tongue and stole my voice

it is a soundless violence

the teaching of shame

the way it coils around bones

i spent my whole life

desperately contorting into

empty spaces and fallen shadows

after all

the smaller the target

the harder it is to hit

right?

it feels like betrayal

when the ones who are supposed

to stitch us back together

become the reason we need

so much damn string

in the first place

doubt presses itself against my throat

i have become a house of cards

balancing inside this shivering cage

i've cried oceans

for so many people

who never even deserved a puddle

there is a war within my blood

some days

it makes me warrior

other days

i am wreckage

it passes

in painstaking minutes

and voiceless sobs

it passes

(when panic overwhelms)

this breath is escaping my lungs

and i remain trapped inside myself

how i crave to be air tonight

if only my insides had wings

(sometimes we are all just human cages)

anxiety can be an unforgiving creature

splitting you open

to pick at your bones

it is the panic stealing my breath

that makes me want to crawl

out of myself and run

i am a gallery of overthinking

each exhibit an almost

a maybe

a should have

artwork in spirals and

late nights that turn into

early mornings and

the kind of regret

that chokes

some days my body itches

to reopen scars

just to feel something real

(a confession)

i have broken my bones

over and over

in this compressing

this folding in upon myself

(i am making an art out of the way

we hide under our skin)

what contradiction

this aching becomes

when sadness is screaming

when it reaches with enthusiastic hands

to tear into flesh and claw at ribs

when it is so loud

that it looks like stillness

in the chaos

there is a part of me that

yearns for metal and

the blooming of crimson

against my skin

(this is how i understand madness)

some nights

when you're raw and bleeding

ripped open again

you'll want to stop feeling

to grow claws and walls and

hide the keys to a thousand locks

but please

do not let this pain take

the soft from you

(your open heart is so very powerful)

there is a hollowness in my lungs

it is the kind that grows

expands until it suffocates

it is a false living

of glass smiles pieced

back together with duct tape

and counterfeit laughter

doled out like monopoly money

the kind of pretending that

makes a skilled liar

(i almost convince myself that i am ok)

this body i live in

does not feel like mine anymore

there is a weariness that

finds its way into your blood

it is the kind that haunts

that throbs like a bruise

i don't remember

the breathing before

drowning stung my lungs

or the way my body settled

before it learned how to shake

or the way this living felt before shame

feel it pouring from your soul

in salt water bleeding

this hurt makes rivers out of us

it is not always

gasping sobs and flashbacks

sometimes it's sadness and stillness

and nothing but the spiralling

thoughts in your head and your

own voice whispering

"sink"

i've grown tired of

lighting matches to keep

the shadows at bay

it wears at your heart

this haunting helplessness

this desperate shrinking

the idea that you are

too much to love

so i sit alone with myself

with my quivering hands

and tired soul

and remember

there used to be a home

between these bones

my body has become a shipwreck

overwhelmed by sweeping waves

swallowed whole and rusting

under the weight of feeling

this breaking does not come

with an instruction manual

Returning

this is where it began

with wobbling limbs

and a tired heart

and waking up one morning

to the realisation that

i didn't want to live

like this anymore

i searched for peace in the destruction

frantic and desperate

turning over rocks until my hands bled

it is time i search for it

in kinder places

i took my first step into

uncertainty on scraped palms

and rattling kneecaps

more parts fear than faith

and moving forward

(still)

let it hurt

in waves rolling through you

scream and cry and sink

under this ocean

i promise the drowning is not eternal

the water settles

the waves ease

and you float back to the surface

(this is how very alive you are)

exhale in the drowning

inhale in the wreckage

you are deconstructed

not destroyed

this is not your end

this is another beginning

through this relearning

this howling resurrection

i hope you meet yourself

i hope you smile when you do

there is a revolution

igniting inside of me

setting fire to my soul

turning this doubt to ash

its consuming me

burning steadily

screaming

"love yourself"

forgive yourself

it is time for your body

to be your home again

i will make petals from this pain

in shades of breathing colour

something beautiful will grow from this

and even on the hardest nights

the earth will still turn

your heart will still beat

and the sun will rise again tomorrow

(these overlooked mercies)

take a step towards the light

i promise

this world will not crumble

if you choose to love yourself

i am clawing my way out of this fear

prying open its teeth in

small stubborn inches

i am making ladders of

what once swallowed me

(i found courage in climbing)

wash away the hours

let the water carry your tears home

let it erase this torment from your skin

let it calm your quaking soul

hear it echo as it falls around you

"you're ok"

"you made it through another day"

and on the trembling nights

gather up this moonlight

into your arms

let it teach you

what it means to glow

despite the dark

do not be ashamed of

your jagged edges

your cracks and broken pieces

fall in love with the parts of yourself

they say don't fit

you are the only one who decides

how you are put together

you are under no obligation

to apologise for your survival

to people who do not try

to understand your war

there are nights i crumble

under the immensity of feeling

and mornings i must

cobble myself back together

speak to yourself in kindness

let it be the only language

your body remembers

this is how your soul

will untangle

find a mirror

stand in front of it and stare

drink in the courage of your smile

the way your eyes light up

the way your skin calls home

drink in the atoms and stardust

and miracle that had to come

together at the right time

to form you

(this is so much more than merely beautiful)

it is not as simple as it sounds

to pack away the bad habits

into boxes and lock the

attic door shut

keys have a way of finding me

(i am learning how to hold them)

(how not to use them)

sometimes healing is in the

unlocking of your bones and

how you must teach them

to walk away from

what hurt you

i'm learning this mending

from my skin

the way it forgives itself in scars

it is a choice i must make

everyday

wither or grow

surrender or fight

revert or recover

mending never promised to be comfortable

(choosing yourself is not always easy)

so stand up and fight

for every moment they said you couldn't

and every moment you knew you could

because you deserve to be fought for

with this armour against your survival skin

prepare for battle

(you are worth so much more than a forfeit)

i built a house of matchsticks

around the doubt hiding

in the dark of me

and with steady hands

and shuddering fingers

i set it on fire

it is in the burning

the way we walk

defiantly on ashes

that we allow ourselves

to shamelessly unbind

it is not painless to rewrite

the words that have been

etched into my bones

yet i think

it is the kind of hurt

worth enduring

give yourself permission to let go

this freedom comes with

the unclenching of fingers

it was one of those trembling days

the kind that bleeds darkness

where my thoughts spiral

and control slips down

the rabbit hole

it was a trying day

where going back feels easier

than fighting and it takes

everything in me not to

crawl into the past

it was a bad day

the kind that shrinks my

lungs with old aching

and erases any memory

of progress

it was one of those

trembling

trying

bad

days

as the day drew to a close

i draped a warm blanket

around my soul

and whispered

"rest"

breathe

broken skin or bone or heart

stitches do not become scars overnight

healing will always take time

weightlessness does not come easy

for souls so used to gravity

it gets heavier before it gets lighter

(but it does)

(and it feels like flying)

i am still trying

to breathe this war

from my lungs

there are lighthouse keepers

whose light will always guide you home

when you are lost to the water

these are the hearts you should treasure

(how lucky we are to know them)

i am writing love letters to myself

of living and feeling and mending

tucking them into stray pockets

reminders for the times resolve is

a wall of crumbling bricks and

i can't remember why i started

(for peace and friends and love)

(for sunrises and words and the ocean)

(for me)

there are still times

fear becomes forest fire

settling alight everything

i've worked to grow

these are moments of slow breaths

and stubborn conviction

(i will bloom again)

somewhere inside the flooding

there is a pause

the kind of exhale

i have been searching for

it happened slowly

in a kind of unnoticeable quiet

like the way ice melts against

the walls of a glass

(how the light whispered to my creases)

(how i became this unfolding)

my body has forgiven me

for so much self-destruction

carefully wiping my tears

smoothing my hair and

stitching itself back together

the silverware doesn't look

like weaponry so much these days

and though i remain in battle

this is victory

(these small steps forward)

homesickness can be a throbbing thing

when the familiarity of darkness

haunts the space beneath your ribs

so when it calls

remember you burned that home down

for a reason

(remember that it was burning you)

i built a fire in my soul

the kind that refuses to be put out

(it warms the rattling out of my bones)

the steps you take

in search of yourself

will not always be

in the right direction

(forgive yourself for the wrong turns)

when this living weighs

heavy against me

i close my eyes

and feel the air

it is only a series of

inhales and exhales

sometimes the words are rivers

that lead me to the edges of this ocean

to feelings i have not yet discovered

i am building doorways into

the walls between my soft

i have found peace

exists in the opening

it felt like home

the way the ocean swam against my body

as i studied the stubbornness of waves

breaking and returning

only to rise again

i can see it

in soft rays of light

and possibility

wading towards me

through the aching

oh

what this life could be

i can see it

some moments grip

they are the kind that wipe

the dust from my heart

that wrench the curtains open

and all at once

this is now

(and i am here)

you'll find it in ways you don't expect

at 1 in the morning

playing board games with friends who feel like family

and real conversation about the kinds of things

that only feel safe to talk about at night

you'll find it in good books

and movie marathons and smiling at

strangers and the way the sun paints colours

into the sky every night

maybe its extraordinary

most of the time it's not

but i swear its real

(happy waits for you in the ordinary)

what gentle mercy

this homecoming

the way my insides settle

with every inhale

Rising

i found my heart poured out in ink

pressed between the pages of old notebooks

that patiently held these lost parts of me

find beauty in your wreckage

pour love into the pieces of yourself

that have never known what that feels like

(make yourself whole)

you will find love in other hearts

so it is easy to forget

it waits for you inside your own

(this human searching)

hope has taken root

blooming

growing

reaching

extending like arms to

wrap itself around me

and isn't it something?

the way i convince myself

the air is gone

only to find these poems

once tucked between my ribs

are gently pulling my lungs open

(the way this body has saved me

time and time again)

my dear girl

find comfort in your skin

fall in love with the colours of you

they will bring you home to yourself

it is in this nurture of my bones

i've learned the difference

between house and home

(these old locks have new keys)

honesty cradles my heart

letting itself become the beat

it is in this that i meet myself

barefaced and naked

it is in this that living becomes truth

(it is in this kind kind mercy)

the freedom brings uncertainty

it is ok not to remain

steady in its wake

they never leave me

the whispers of disorder

there are days

they overwhelm again

and try to tempt me

and days i do not

hear them at all

(my healing is in learning how not to listen)

your past is not your present

your present is not your future

(this life is transitioning)

my body is not a problem to be solved

i am a perfect square

a series of derivatives and curves

interconnected by blood and bone

i am not an equation

waiting for someone else

to find the answer

some days i drift

quietly

lazily

the way clouds pass

against blue skies

relishing every taste of relearning

(these floating homes)

i am attaching stop signs

to certain trains of thought

which is to say

that i am learning

there was something about the horizon

the way the sky arched down to reach the sea

the way the deep stretched endlessly to meet it

there is comfort there

in the meeting of wonders

it feels like a place where miracles could exist

how humbling

the patience of bones

the kindness of skin

and the resilience of organs

(there is gratitude in my blood these days)

beautiful is in you

but it is not beautiful that makes you

(this is a lesson i am still learning)

i am born of screaming women

their echoes are in my blood

i will deafen anyone

who tries to silence me

there is light today

bright and yearning

don't you feel it?

this quiet revolution

this starlit freedom

longing to be yours

trembling

just beneath your fingertips

i am finding artistry

in the lines of my body

the curves flowing

around my bones

the shame is leaving this creation

oh

the way the earth

breaks cracks into concrete

just to taste the air

this is how survival meets living

(in small breaths of bravery)

there is powerful magic

in loving yourself

(why do you think the world tries

so hard to stop you?)

shame has a way of bending

itself into shadows and looking

like a trick of the light

but i have become a huntress

inside this body and these

arrows can see through the dark

she didn't realise she was on fire

until someone tried to put her out

(you hold more power than you know)

the mercy

seeps into my skin

like honey dissolving

in tea

(it is the sweetest relief)

there are lessons tucked

into every piece of me

i have recollected

i'm teaching them to myself

every night

(i am rebuilt in these bedtime stories)

i am a work in progress

threaded by this living

sewn together and unravelling

at once

it is a terribly wonderful contradiction

to be so whole and trembling

and desperately alive

the absence of destruction

leaves a silence

where even whispers echo

this is the power of a voice

(you can fill it on your own)

my resurrection was not beautiful

it was bleeding knuckles

ripped earth

and burning skin

it was smoke-filled lungs

and screaming

it was not beautiful

but oh

it was some kind of miracle

i have fought for this feeling

for this breath in my lungs and

this forgiveness in my blood

there are parts of me

that will never forget

the taste of torment

sometimes it lingers

just beneath my tongue

and that is ok

i am learning what

happiness tastes like too

i hope you fall

desperately

irretrievably

wonderfully

in love with living

(this life is yours)

my heart is a wild thing

roaring and unapologetic

i am learning i cannot change

the way it feels in tidal waves

i am learning there is relief

in letting the ocean free

i built a home

out of my broken pieces

this weary skeleton is a healing foundation

(there is shelter here now)

doubt waits for the wobbling moments

for loss and uncertainty and wrong turns

the inevitable potholes in this road

it is not easy to protect your heart

when it is breaking

(remember you have rebuilt before)

(remember the doubt lies)

dig your toes in

find your roots

sometimes you need to remember

there is safety under the ground

when the fall from the branches

feel too high

the path feels like life

pressing itself up against my feet

this is how i know it is not a finish line

(may i always be this endless learning)

there is a stillness anchored here now

it rests in the corners of me

expanding quietly

to temper the fluttering

i was born a daughter of Zeus

a daughter of Thor

i am rolling thunder rounding into

crescendos of lightning bolts stretched

across this skin

a walking electric storm

(this is the power of holding fire in mortal hands)

listen for the gentle thunder

echoing under your skin

the quiet reminder

that you are made of more

sometimes

i am softness and stillness and

dancing with the air against me

others

i am sharp and shaking and

stumbling into a pile on my bed

most of the time i am both

which is to say that

i am still a mess

part healing

part havoc

and all so wonderfully human

cherish the way your body

curves and stretches

spilling softly against your bones

let it remind you

to never make yourself small

for anyone again

i unravelled the ocean of me

let it escape in rolling waves and undertow

no longer willing to live in shrinking

these are the kinds of tides

that demand to be heard

i am afraid of many things

that claw into the softness of me

and still i let life into my lungs

and still i am brave

endings have a way of leaving scars sometimes

they are the kind that speak in aching

and teach lessons in letting go

still

i am grateful to have held them

like raindrops and seasons and time

there is something beautiful in

the way it is all temporary

(there are infinite beginnings inside of us)

it was a petal soft daydream

held between cupped palms

a hopeful forgiveness

that found its way into my heart

it was this

unrestrained laughter

easy breathing

and a heart beating

open curtains streaming sunlight

burning boldly bright

it was something like kindness

and a lot like love

(the shedding of shame)

i replaced my swords with stems

grew flowers where there

was once bloodshed

made fields of forgiveness

out of this battlefield heart

it is new

this lightness

this sun kissed weightlessness

holding my heart in champagne bubbles

i know i can't regret it

any aching second

because somehow

despite everything

i became my own again

to feel like this

wholly

unrestrained

spilling over the edges

it is the way

i can hold lightning in my hands

and not look for bottles

the way i can fall so in love

with living that it has begun to

ease the fear

(oh to be so full)

press your fingers

to your pulse

and feel it

the life in you

(still)

there are spaces between my bones

that still hold this trembling

that still flood when the waves crash

leaving behind salt stains

and the echoes of aching

and that is ok

there are parts of us that are meant

to shake and quiver and thrash

against this current

it is not human to be

entirely still in this tide

i believe there is growing in me still

that it is only ever

the ebb and flow of our ocean hearts

in movement

but today

oh today

i let the air into these garden lungs

and remember just how much

blooming i have done

(it still feels like miracle)

About the author

nimasha d weerakoon (pen name: n dumindi) is a
Sri-Lankan Australian writer and poet, whose words
are her doorway to understanding the soft shattering
of this life. she currently lives in Melbourne and shares
her time between studying and creating, often finding
herself writing poetry in between lecture notes.

she can be found on instagram (@nd.poetry).

Ocean Hearts

N. Dumindi

ISBN: 9780648327745   Qty

RRP   AU$19.99   .....

Postage within Australia   AU$5.00   .....

TOTAL* $_____

* All prices include GST

Name: ....

Address: ....

....

Phone: ....

Email: ....

Payment: [ ] Money Order   [ ] Cheque   [ ] MasterCard   [ ]Visa

Cardholder's Name:..

Credit Card Number: ....

Signature:..

Expiry Date: ....

Allow 7 days for delivery.

Payment to: Marzocco Consultancy (ABN 14 067 257 390)

PO Box 12544

A'Beckett Street, Melbourne, 8006

Victoria, Australia

admin@brolgapublishing.com.au

Be Published

Publish through a successful publisher.
Brolga Publishing is represented through:
• National book trade distribution, including sales,
marketing & distribution through Dennis Jones and
Associates Australia.
• International book trade distribution to:
  - The United Kingdom
  - North America
  - Sales representation in South East Asia
• Worldwide e-Book distribution

For details and enquiries, contact:
Brolga Publishing Pty Ltd
PO Box 12544
A'Beckett St
Melbourne, Vic 8006
markzocchi@brolgapublishing.com.au
(Email for a catalogue request)